Hero

A Play

Michael Lynch

Samuel French – London
New York – Sydney – Toronto – Hollywood

Copyright © 1986 by Samuel French Ltd
All Rights Reserved

HERO is fully protected under the copyright laws of the British Commonwealth, including Canada, the United States of America, and all other countries of the Copyright Union. All rights, including professional and amateur stage productions, recitation, lecturing, public reading, motion picture, radio broadcasting, television and the rights of translation into foreign languages are strictly reserved.

ISBN 978-0-573-12089-3

www.samuelfrench.co.uk

www.samuelfrench.com

For Amateur Production Enquiries

United Kingdom and World excluding North America

plays@samuelfrench.co.uk

020 7255 4302/01

Each title is subject to availability from Samuel French, depending upon country of performance.

CAUTION: Professional and amateur producers are hereby warned that *HERO* is subject to a licensing fee. Publication of this play does not imply availability for performance. Both amateurs and professionals considering a production are strongly advised to apply to the appropriate agent before starting rehearsals, advertising, or booking a theatre. A licensing fee must be paid whether the title is presented for charity or gain and whether or not admission is charged.

No one shall make any changes in this title for the purpose of production. No part of this book may be reproduced, stored in a retrieval system, or transmitted in any form, by any means, now known or yet to be invented, including mechanical, electronic, photocopying, recording, videotaping, or otherwise, without the prior written permission of the publisher. No one shall upload this title, or part of this title, to any social media websites.

The right of Michael Lynch to be identified as author of this work has been asserted in accordance with Section 77 of the Copyright, Designs and Patents Act 1988.

HERO

First performed at the Little Theatre, Leicester with the following cast of characters:

Captain Selkirk   Michael Lloyd
Sister Hart   Margaret Stone
Nurse Penfold   Naomi Shuttlewood
Private Underwood   Christopher Mills

Directed by Ted Sharpe

The action of the play takes place in a small British casualty clearing station close to the lines on the Western Front

Time—1916

SUGGESTED COSTUME

Selkirk: white coat over officer's uniform

Sister Hart: 1914–18 nursing uniform, cap and apron

Nurse Penfold: 1914–18 nursing uniform, cap and apron

Private Underwood: body heavily bandaged, head and face fully visible

HERO*

A small British casualty clearing station close to the lines on the Western Front—1916

The station is housed in little more than a large canvas tent. A number of beds are suggested but only one need be authentic. There is a chair and table or cabinet by the bed. Medical equipment is lying around the room. There is a storm lantern hanging from the roof. A roughly curtained off area serves as the M.O.'s office. There is a table, with drawer, and a chair in the centre of the area. Books, files and papers are all across the table and there is also a storm lantern placed on the table. A folding stool is stored in the corner

The deafening roar of an artillery barrage precedes the opening of the play, this fades to give place to bird song which then fades in turn

Intermittently throughout the play the rumble of gunfire, with the occasional loud salvo, can be heard

As the CURTAIN *rises the Lights come up to daylight. Captain Selkirk is sitting in the M.O.'s office. Private Ralph Underwood is in bed in the ward. Sister Hart crosses the stage and is about to pass the M.O.'s office when Captain Selkirk calls out to her*

Selkirk Sister, have you a moment?
Sister Of course, sir. (*She turns back and enters the office*)
Selkirk I just wanted to check that you had enough supplies before I send in the order. (*He points to the papers on his desk*) Or do you think you'll be able to manage on what you have?
Sister Provided we have no fresh casualties we can cope for three or four days. Are we likely to be heavily pressed, sir?
Selkirk We cannot be certain, of course, but I'm hopeful that with the enemy's offensive petering out our numbers will be bearable ... at least for the time being. How are your nurses taking the strain, Sister?
Sister They know their duty, sir.
Selkirk Quite so, Sister. They all seem very experienced. (*Trying*

---

*N.B. Paragraph 3 on page ii of this Acting Edition regarding photocopying and video-recording should be carefully read.

to make it appear an after-thought) Although there is one I didn't recognize. She seems a little younger than the others.

Sister That, I think, would be Nurse Penfold, sir. She joined us only three days ago. I understand she is newly qualified.

Selkirk Thrown in at the deep end, eh? One day here is equivalent to a lifetime's experience back in England.

Sister Very true, sir.

Selkirk There isn't much she won't know about life—or death—after she has been here a little while.

Sister She did volunteer, sir.

Selkirk Most of us did, Sister. It doesn't make it any easier, conscripted or not.

Sister No, sir.

Selkirk God knows, I've seen enough misery and death to become immune to it all but there are still moments when I find it almost impossible to take. ... So you and your nurses never cease to excite my sympathy, Sister.

Sister (*coldly*) Thank you, sir.

Selkirk And my admiration!

Sister (*scarcely warmer*) Thank you, sir.

Selkirk Sister, I would like a brief word with your new nurse. Just to welcome her, let her know she's been noticed.

Sister Nurse Penfold, sir?

Selkirk Yes, that's right.

Sister Very well, sir.

Selkirk You don't approve?

Sister It isn't my place to say, sir.

Selkirk But you still don't approve?

Sister Since you ask me, sir, I will simply say that I prefer my nurses to be more mature. Nursing is at its best when it is detached.

Selkirk And you feel the young cannot distance themselves sufficiently?

Sister There is that danger.

Selkirk I'm afraid this war does not allow us to pick and choose anymore.

Sister I'm sure you're right, sir. I'll ask Nurse Penfold to come and see you, shall I, sir?

Selkirk If you would be so good, Sister.

Sister Hart leaves the office and crosses the ward again. Captain Selkirk continues with his paper work

Sister (*calling off*) Nurse Penfold, would you leave what you are doing for a moment, please!
Nurse (*off*) Yes, Sister.

Nurse Penfold enters

Yes, Sister?
Sister Captain Selkirk would like to see you, Nurse.
Nurse Now, Sister?
Sister Yes, now. I'll finish changing those dressings. You had better run along.

Nurse Penfold starts to go

And Nurse...
Nurse Yes, Sister?
Sister Don't stay too long.
Nurse But, Sister——
Sister I know, you can stay only as long as Captain Selkirk keeps you. What I mean is, don't ask him any questions or give overlong answers. He has a lot of work to do—so have you, Nurse, so don't encroach on his time. Understand?
Nurse Yes, Sister.

Sister Hart exits offstage

Nurse Penfold crosses to the office, pulls back the curtained door and coughs to gain Captain Selkirk's attention

You wanted to see me, sir?
Selkirk Ah, yes; Nurse Penfold, isn't it?
Nurse That's right, sir.
Selkirk Please come in and sit down. (*He assembles the folding stool*)

Nurse Penfold enters the office and sits on the folding stool

I wanted to take the chance to welcome you to the hospital here.
Nurse Thank you, sir.
Selkirk I realize it isn't exactly Bart's but you'll certainly learn your nursing here. I haven't had time to welcome you before but

I don't need to tell you how busy we've been these last few days. Now, Sister tells me you've just qualified?

Nurse Yes, sir, two months ago.

Selkirk Two months? You haven't wasted any time.

Nurse I put in for a French posting as soon as I knew I was going to qualify.

Selkirk Keen to do your bit, eh?

Nurse I wanted to help as best I could, yes sir.

Selkirk No regrets?

Nurse None so far, sir.

Selkirk You haven't been revolted by what you have seen?

Nurse Not revolted, no sir.

Selkirk Angered, perhaps?

Nurse Angered, sir?

Selkirk Yes, you must have felt some reaction when you saw all this death, this misery, this waste. No?

Nurse I had been well briefed before I left England, sir.

Selkirk So you were prepared for the shock?

Nurse Yes, sir.

Selkirk I find that remarkable. I've been running a military hospital for two years, almost as long as the war itself, but I'm still shocked and angered almost daily. In fact, I sometimes think it's the anger that makes the job bearable. That surprises you, doesn't it?

Nurse Sir?

Selkirk Scientific detachment—that's what you expect isn't it? That's what they told you in training. Sister is a firm believer in detachment. She believes it makes for good nursing—and who am I to challenge her, she's been in medicine longer than I have. This is a strange sort of hospital, Nurse. It's very much a transit camp. If the men are going to recover we patch them up and send them back to England, if they're not we keep them here until they die. So we never actually cure anyone. That can be very depressing if you let it. Will you let it depress you, Nurse?

Nurse I hope not, sir.

Selkirk Yes, this hospital began life as little more than a dressing station. At first there were no female nurses, only orderlies. But once it became clear this war wasn't going to be over quickly we became permanently established and the top brass let us have a

few nurses. However, I expect you've already been told enough about the history of this place so I won't bore you with details. I just wanted to introduce myself and say welcome aboard.
Nurse Thank you, sir.
Selkirk And to say that if you have any difficulties, nursing or personal, please don't be afraid to approach me.
Nurse Thank you, sir.
Selkirk As to the nursing, there is one case I would like you to pay special attention to—the one in bed number nine. Has Sister mentioned him to you?
Nurse Not directly, sir, but is it the soldier who was brought in earlier this morning?
Selkirk That's right, just an hour or two ago. The poor devil tried to walk here on his own, he didn't make it, of course. When the stretcher-party found him he was lying in the road. They thought he was already dead.
Nurse He won't last long, then, sir?
Selkirk No, twelve hours or so at the most. I've done what I can for him but there's no point sending him on anywhere else, he wouldn't survive the journey. I would be grateful if you could spare him a little extra time. Dying isn't difficult, it's the loneliness they can't bear.
Nurse I'll do my best, sir.
Selkirk Thank you, I know you will. I think that will be all for the moment, Nurse, thank you.
Nurse Thank you, sir. (*She makes to go*)
Selkirk Oh, Nurse, just one more thing.
Nurse Yes, sir?
Selkirk You don't drink, do you?
Nurse Drink ... ? No, sir, I don't.
Selkirk Good. Mr Lloyd George would be very pleased to hear that. Well, goodbye for the present, Nurse, and thank you again. (*He smiles broadly at her*)
Nurse (*uncertain how to take him*) Thank you, sir.

Nurse Penfold exits from the office and crosses the ward. Captain Selkirk waits a moment, smiling, he takes a metal flask from a drawer in his table and drinks

Sister Hart enters and meets Nurse Penfold

Sister There you are, Nurse. I hope you didn't outstay your welcome?

Nurse No, Sister, I left as soon as Captain Selkirk dismissed me.

Sister (*with the merest hint of sarcasm*) Of course you did. Let me ask you, Nurse; did Captain Selkirk suggest that you should go to him with any difficulties you might encounter here?

Nurse (*hesitantly*) Yes, Sister ... he did.

Sister Naturally you will never attempt to take advantage of that suggestion.

Nurse I'm sorry, Sister, I don't understand.

Sister Then let me make myself perfectly clear, Nurse Penfold; you are here to perform the duty for which you were trained—to nurse and care for the wounded patients in this hospital—nothing more and nothing less. Socializing with other members of the staff here is not among your duties.

Nurse But, Sister, I only——

Sister (*cutting in*) I think I can anticipate what you are going to say, Nurse; you did not ask to speak to Captain Selkirk, he sent for you. That is quite true. What I am pointing out is that that was a matter of courtesy; you are not to presume any further on that courtesy by approaching him as he suggested. Captain Selkirk is an exceptionally able doctor but, as you cannot be unaware, he is also extremely busy. You will not help him by going to him with impertinent questions. Should you have any problems you will, of course, raise them with me. Have I made myself clear, Nurse Penfold?

Nurse Perfectly, Sister.

Sister Very well. Now let us return to our nursing. I have finished the dressings on your last patient. I would like you now to take particular care of the patient in bed nine. He was brought in a short while ago. He——

Nurse Yes, Sister, Captain Selkirk asked me to look after him.

Sister Did he now? Then you will know that the new patient is failing fast. I am asking that you keep this in mind when you are with him; he may need a little more time than the others.

Nurse Yes, Sister.

Sister You are not, of course, to neglect the other patients in any way.

Nurse No, Sister.

Sister Very well. I now suggest it is high time you went back to your duties.

Nurse Yes, Sister.

Sister Hart exits offstage

Nurse Penfold goes slowly across to bed nine occupied by the terminal case. She stands for some time looking down at the apparently sleeping figure. While this is taking place Captain Selkirk breaks off temporarily from his paperwork to take another long draught from his flask. Eventually Nurse Penfold reaches out and touches the man's shoulder. Private Underwood turns slightly to look up at her. We see him clearly for the first time, he is young, pale and tousled

You are awake, then?

Ralph *(suggestion of a West-Country burr)* Yes, miss, I'm awake.

Nurse *(looking at his treatment sheet)* And you are Private Ralph Underwood?

Ralph That's it, miss, Private Ralph Underwood, ten-sixty-four-nine-thirty-two, reporting for duty.

Nurse *(laughing softly)* Do you feel any pain, Private Ralph?

Ralph It comes and goes, miss; there are times, like now, when I can't feel anything at all.

Nurse That's good. And are you comfortable?

Ralph It'll do. It's more comfortable, any road, than I've known these last few days.

Nurse They said you were trying to walk here. Is that right?

Ralph Yes, miss, I was. I suppose it was a bit of a daft thing to do. But I've always loved walking and after I was hit, although I knew I was hurt bad, I wanted to walk even more. So when the barrage stopped I just got up and started walking... I've always liked walking... at home I walk a lot.

Nurse And where is home, soldier boy?

Ralph Tiverton; I work with my dad on his farm there.

Nurse Do you like working on a farm?

Ralph Yes, I do very much.

Nurse Then you must be missing it?

Ralph I am—a lot. I don't like it here in France.

Nurse Never mind, perhaps you will soon be home.

Ralph Do you know what I miss most of all? The birds singing. There aren't any birds here. That's because there aren't any trees or hedges left.

He is suddenly racked with pain; he gasps and writhes. When the spasm subsides she takes a flannel from a basin on the chair, wrings it, and gently wipes his face. He relaxes

"Thou shalt purge me with hyssop, and I shall be clean: thou shalt wash me, and I shall be whiter than snow."

Nurse (*surprised*) My, that has a fine sound to it! Where did you learn that?

Ralph It must have been in church, miss; I used to be in the choir. It's Psalm fifty-one.

Nurse Is it now? And what is hyssop?

Ralph Strange you should ask that, miss; I've always wondered myself ever since I first heard the minister read it out. Hyssop... it's a wonderful word. I'm going to try some one day. I've really got to, whatever it is.

Nurse (*gently mocking*) Hadn't you better find out what it is first?

Ralph I suppose so but I know it's something good, I just know.

Nurse Well, I haven't any hyssop, I'm afraid, but perhaps you would like a little water?

Ralph Please.

Nurse Penfold pours water from a jug into an enamel mug; supporting his head with one hand she holds the mug to his lips. It is only with the greatest difficulty that he drinks. While he does so we are conscious of Captain Selkirk again swigging from his flask

Sister Hart enters with a requisition form and stares across at bed nine

Nurse Penfold puts the mug down, she adjusts the pillows and lays his head back

Nurse There now—comfortable?

Private Underwood nods

I'm just going to slip away and look at my other patients.

Private Underwood, with surprising strength, grabs Nurse Penfold's hand and holds it tightly, there is a look of fear in his eyes. She puts a finger to her lips, the way one would quieten a fretful child. He relaxes

I shan't be long.

She leaves the bedside and is about to cross the ward when Sister Hart stops her

Sister Nurse Penfold, one moment.
Nurse (*going to her*) Yes, Sister?
Sister Nurse, you will doubtless recall what I said to you in my introductory talk when you first arrived?
Nurse Sister?
Sister Let me remind you. I was at pains to point out the danger confronting us of becoming too close to our patients. We do neither them nor ourselves a service if we allow them, through an excess of sympathy, to become dependent on us. To avoid this I insist that all my nurses maintain as formal an approach to the patients as good nursing permits. Good nursing does not include the use of Christian names or unnecessary physical contact. Nurse, when I asked you to pay extra attention to that patient (*she motions towards Private Underwood*) I simply meant that because of his critical condition he would require more time and care; I was not asking you to enter into familiarity.

Sister Hart, seeing that Nurse Penfold has stiffened, softens her tone a little

Nurse, I assure you that what I am saying is for the best. Our work is never easy, especially in a hospital like this. Remember that we are often the first women these soldiers will have seen for some time; if our brief meetings and partings are not to become pathetic we must remain detached. A degree of formality helps to make our work and their suffering more endurable. I hope I have persuaded you, Nurse?

Nurse (*with a manifest effort*) Yes, Sister.
Sister I am pleased and I think your other patients are waiting, Nurse.
Nurse Yes, Sister.

Nurse Penfold exits offstage

Sister Hart watches her going and then crosses to the M.O.'s office

Sister (*calling from outside*) Captain Selkirk!
Selkirk Is that you, Sister. Please come in. (*He is concerned with putting the flask in the drawer out of sight*)
Sister (*entering*) Excuse me, sir; I've checked our stock and the only urgent need is for more ether and morphine. We are still reasonably well supplied for most of the other things. (*She hands him the requisition form*)

Selkirk Right, thank you, Sister. (*He places the requisition on top of a pile of papers*) I never seem quite able to keep up with the administration of all this.

Sister Perhaps, sir, now that there is something of a lull in the fighting I might be able to spare one of the nurses to help clear the paper work.

Selkirk I'm sorry, Sister, I wasn't meaning to drop hints. Thank you, all the same, but I think your nurses have more than enough to do without their being bothered attending to red tape. No, I'll get it done eventually and, if not, then H.Q. will just have to whistle for it. Do you think they know there's a war on, Sister?

Sister (*declining to share his levity*) I am sure they do, sir.

Selkirk Yes, of course. ... Well, Sister, I had a word with your new nurse; she is very young, as you said, but she struck me as being quite responsible and she seems keen enough. Do you think she will make the grade, Sister?

Sister I am confident that with time and experience Nurse Penfold will develop into a capable member of our profession.

Selkirk (*jocularly*) I'm sure a few days under your gentle tutelage will bring out the best in her, Sister.

Sister (*still refusing to be humoured*) Let us hope so, sir. I understand you suggested she should take care of Private Underwood?

Selkirk Ah, yes, Underwood. That's right, Sister, they're both about the same age so I thought he would appreciate being nursed by someone like her. A bit of companionship is about all we can offer him; there's precious little else we can do for the poor fellow. You didn't mind my suggesting that, Sister?

Sister (*icily*) Of course not, sir ...

There is an awkward silence

If there is nothing else, sir ...

Selkirk No, no, not for the present, thank you for bringing your requisition so promptly, Sister.

Sister Hart starts to go

(*Standing*) Sister.

Sister Hart turns back

You don't suppose H.Q. would send us a crate of whisky if I put in for one?
Sister I very much doubt it, Captain Selkirk.
Selkirk So do I, Sister, so do I. . . . Thank you again, Sister.
Sister Thank you, sir.

Sister Hart leaves the office and exits offstage

Captain Selkirk sits down wearily in his chair and reaches resignedly for his flask. He drinks

The Lights fade slowly, to denote the passing of some hours, and then come up again. It is darker now, the day is drawing to a close

Nurse Penfold is at Private Underwood's bedside, she is spooning soup into his mouth. He dribbles with each spoonful. Meticulously she wipes him each time with a towel

Nurse A little more?

Private Underwood shakes his head

Then let's lean back shall we? (*She puts down the soup bowl and towel*) There now. (*She adjusts his pillows and lays him back*)
Ralph Thank you, miss.

Nurse Penfold begins wiping his face and neck with a flannel

Do you know, miss, I still don't know your name.
Nurse Yes, you do, it's Nurse Penfold.
Ralph But your first name?
Nurse (*teasingly*) Nurses are not required to be on first name terms with their patients.
Ralph Oh, sorry I'm sure.
Nurse . . . It's Veronica.
Ralph (*almost with reverence*) Veronica Penfold . . . Veronica . . . that's got a lovely sound.
Nurse As lovely as hyssop?

They both laugh. He is seized with pain, she comforts him by taking both his hands in hers. When the spasm has passed she again bathes his face and holds the cup to his lips. He takes a few sips, then relaxes

Ralph "Thou has anointed my head with oil and my cup runneth over."

Nurse Another of your quotations? The Psalms again?
Ralph Yes, Psalm twenty-three: "Yea, though I walk through the shadow of the valley of death ..."
Nurse (*taking it up*) "... I will fear no evil for thou art with me."
Ralph You know it, too?
Nurse Only odd bits, not much more than that really. (*She takes his hand*)

They look at each other without speaking

The Lights fade slowly and then come up again, it is late evening and the lanterns are lit

Captain Selkirk is examining Private Underwood, with great care. Sister Hart is on the other side of the bed, assisting. After some time the examination is finished. Leaving Sister Hart to tidy the sheets and resettle the patient Captain Selkirk comes away from the bed. Her tidying done, Sister Hart re-joins him. Captain Selkirk shakes his head

Selkirk He won't see through the night. It's now simply a question of how much morphine we give him, a shorter, less painful end against a longer, agonized one. Doesn't a man have a right to be conscious during his last hours, Sister?
Sister No matter how anguished those hours are, sir?
Selkirk Is that the solution, pump him full of morphine so that he doesn't feel a thing—just meets his maker earlier than intended?
Sister Isn't our duty ... (*she stops*) ... I'm sorry, sir.
Selkirk No, Sister, please say what you were going to. I'm not beyond advice, God knows.
Sister Well, sir; isn't our professional responsibility to save life and, where we cannot do that, to ease suffering?
Selkirk At the cost of shortening life?
Sister With respect, sir, we don't decide that. That, it seems to me, is God's decision.
Selkirk Maybe, Sister. I just wish He would make His decisions a little easier to interpret, that's all.
Sister Sir, we have faced exactly similar choices practically every day of this war. I do not see ... (*again she stops*)
Selkirk And you don't see why Private Underwood's case should be treated any differently?
Sister Yes, sir, that is what I was going to ask.

Selkirk That's a perfectly fair question. The truth is there's a complication in this case ...

Sister Hart looks puzzled

Sister, I think you should step into my office a moment. There's something you should know.

They cross to Captain Selkirk's office. He ushers Sister Hart in ahead of him, goes to the desk and picks up a piece of paper which he hands to her

This paper was discovered among the effects of the company runner who was dead on arrival when brought here an hour ago. I would like you to read it.

There is a pause whilst Sister Hart reads the letter

Selkirk (*having finished it*) I see. You consider this makes a difference to the way we should treat Private Underwood?
Selkirk I do, Sister. Don't you?
Sister With respect, sir, I don't.
Selkirk You cannot see why we should keep Underwood conscious now as long as possible?
Sister So that he can have charges served on him?
Selkirk And so that he can defend himself.
Sister Again with respect, sir, I would suggest that they are military considerations.
Selkirk This is a military hospital.
Sister Indeed so, sir, but my first duty is to the men as patients not as soldiers.
Selkirk Unfortunately, I do not have the luxury of choosing. I am an officer in His Majesty's armed forces.
Sister Are you not also a doctor, sir?
Selkirk That does not absolve me from obedience to higher authority.
Sister (*after a pause*) Sir, am I to understand that your orders are to cease giving Private Underwood pain-relieving drugs?
Selkirk Yes, those are my orders for the present, Sister Hart.
Sister Very well, sir. You do, of course, appreciate that when the effect of his last injection wears off he will begin to experience the most acute pain.

Selkirk (*snapping*) Dammit, Sister, of course I realize that. I don't need instruction in such matters.
Sister I apologize, sir. I did not mean to challenge your authority.
Selkirk (*recovering himself*) No, Sister, it's I who should apologize, my outburst was uncalled for. It is just that I would like you to understand my reasoning. Underwood has very little time left, if he is comatose for most of that time he will not be able to understand or answer the accusations being made. As a soldier I cannot allow another soldier to die with an unanswered charge of cowardice against him.
Sister Permission to speak, sir.
Selkirk Of course.
Sister I take it the company runner was taking this paper to battalion headquarters when he was killed.
Selkirk Yes, Sister, that's correct.
Sister Am I also right in thinking that all the officers in Private Underwood's platoon were killed in the recent action.
Selkirk Yes, correct again. The bombardment wiped out the whole platoon, Underwood is the only survivor.
Sister Then, sir, there are no living witnesses to Private Underwood's desertion, if such it was, and no written evidence except this document. (*She returns the paper to him*)
Selkirk Are you suggesting I should not forward this paper to H.Q.?
Sister I am suggesting nothing, sir. I am simply pointing out that the officer who wrote that paper and all other witnesses to the action it purports to describe are no longer alive.

The Lights fade slowly and then come up again, it is now night time

Nurse Penfold is tending Private Underwood

Ralph ... after harvesting ... it always seems to rain when the hunt comes across the fields ... their coats are all spashed with mud ... red coats splashed with mud ... mud ... red mud ...

Private Underwood speaks with great difficulty, occasionally retching. Nurse Penfold continually wipes his face and mouth

The Lights crossfade to Captain Selkirk's office

Captain Selkirk is seen pacing in his office, he stops, sprawls wearily in his chair, and then drains what is obviously the last drop from his flask

The Lights crossfade to the ward

Nurse Penfold is still at Private Underwood's bed side

Ralph ... I'm not sure what I like most, the taste of the bread or the smell of it, fresh from the oven ... I know I should have stayed but I think all the others were dead by then ... (*with sudden and loud passion*) I don't like the sound of guns.

Nurse Penfold is quick to comfort him. He relaxes

The Lights fade slowly and then come up again on the ward

Nurse Penfold and Sister Hart are standing away from bed number nine but looking back at it

Sister Yes, Nurse, but at this stage we should, of course, expect delirium. Little of what he says from now on will make much sense. It's very common with badly wounded cases. They talk of having deserted their post; it's as if they feel guilty for being wounded.

The Lights fade slowly and then come up again

Captain Selkirk, Sister Hart and Nurse Penfold are grouped around the bed. Captain Selkirk is finishing his examination of Private Underwood, who is obviously in great discomfort. Captain Selkirk comes away from the bed, having completed the settling of Private Underwood, Sister Hart joins Captain Selkirk leaving Nurse Penfold still tending the patient

Selkirk (*looking knowingly at her*) I would like you to continue with the morphine injections, Sister ... you understand?
Sister Yes, Sir ... thank you, sir.
Selkirk Sister, does Nurse Penfold know about the charges against him?
Sister Not to my knowledge, sir, though in his ramblings Private Underwood seems to have referred to desertion. Would you like me to inform her of the position?
Selkirk Do you think she should be told?
Sister Frankly, no, sir; I do not consider it would help in the circumstances.

Selkirk In that case let us leave matters as they are. ... Thank you, Sister.
Sister Thank you, sir.

After looking back at the bed they both exit in separate directions

During the following ramblings which are interspersed with gasps of pain Nurse Penfold continues to bathe his face, hold and stroke his hands, and generally show affectionate care

Ralph ... doctors can be very gentle ... gentle ... very gentle for a man ... the bottom fields are always the last to drain ... salt keeps meat a long time ... I suppose I ought to have stayed but all the others ... all the others ... they weren't getting up, they couldn't, not most of them ... most of them were dead ... most of them ... they were all splashed with mud ... their coats, their red coats were all splashed ... too many guns, too many guns ... (*loudly*) there are too many guns ... raining, the horses always know when it's going to rain; they hold their heads a different way ... I didn't leave the others, there was nothing else I could do ... they were covered in mud, their coats were all splashed, splashed with mud ... they were sinking in ... (*Suddenly sitting up he becomes cogent*) Miss Veronica, am I going to die?
Nurse (*only a slight pause*) Yes, Ralph, you are going to die.
Ralph (*smiling*) Will it be soon?
Nurse Yes, Ralph, quite soon.
Ralph Days or hours, miss?
Nurse No one can be certain, but hours probably.
Ralph (*pondering, almost detached*) I'm not afraid. I'm dying but I'm not afraid.
Nurse (*laying him back gently*) That's good Ralph, that's very good. Would you like to see the padre?
Ralph No, miss, I don't think so ... I don't think I need to see him, not, that is, if you'll be with me when ... when it happens. Will you be with me? Will you promise?
Nurse Yes, Ralph, I'll be with you, I promise. Try to rest now, I won't leave you.

Sister Hart enters carrying a bowl and syringe. She prepares Private Underwood's arm and injects him

Private Underwood, all the while, gazes intently at Nurse Penfold, who grips his hand

Sister Hart exits

The Lights fade slowly and then come up again

Nurse Penfold is still with Private Underwood. She has just written a letter at his dictation

Ralph Do you think they will like that, miss?
Nurse I know they will, Ralph.
Ralph I've never been very good at writing letters. I always have to ask my mates to help and that makes me feel a bit daft sometimes. But not when I'm with you.
Nurse Lots of people aren't particularly good when it comes to writing letters, it helps to have a stranger give a hand.
Ralph I don't think of you as a stranger, miss.
Nurse (*softly*) That's nice, Ralph. ... Would you like me to read the letter back to you?
Ralph Yes, please, very much.

Nurse Penfold reads, glancing up every so often to check his condition. Rapt, he gazes at her the whole time

Nurse Dear Mum and Dad, I hope you are all well at home. I miss you all very much and often think about you and what you are doing. I know it will be harvesting soon but I am very sorry to tell you that I don't think I shall be there to help you this year. This morning I stopped a rather nasty one and will have to stay in hospital. You are not to worry about me as I am being looked after very well here. Mum and Dad, you have always been very good to me and I want to thank you for all you have done. I am proud to be your son and hope you think the same. This morning the fighting stopped for a little while and then the birds sang and that made me think of you at home very much. If I do not come back you must not be too sad. Your ever loving son, Ralph.
Ralph How beautifully you read!
Nurse You love sounds, don't you, Ralph?
Ralph Yes, I do, Miss Veronica, I do.
Nurse Do you think you can sign it?

Ralph I'll try, miss.

She takes his hand, places the pencil in his limp fingers, and slowly inscribes his name

Nurse There we are, well done.

She replaces his hand under the covers and adjusts his pillows

Ralph I didn't really desert them, did I, miss, not really?

Nurse (*not fully understanding but humouring him*) Of course you didn't, Ralph.

Ralph There was no one left. . . . Their coats were all red. . . . They were all splashed with mud. . . . I've always liked walking. At home I walk a lot. . . . So when the barrage stopped I just got up and started walking. . . . Miss, are the birds still singing?

Nurse Yes, Ralph, they're still singing. (*They are not of course*) Can't you hear them? Listen . . .

Ralph . . . Yes, of course . . . yes, yes . . . I don't think they sing any better than that at home. . . . Miss, will you do something for me?

Nurse Of course, Ralph, if I can.

Ralph . . . Miss . . . will you tell me you love me?

Nurse (*taking his hand in both of hers she raises it to her lips*) . . . Yes, Private Ralph Underwood of Tiverton, lover of birdsong and psalms, I love you . . .

Ralph (*speaking with one last great effort*) "Lord, now lettest thou thy servant depart in peace, according to thy word . . ." (*his voice trails away. He remains smiling at her but is slipping into unconsciousness*)

The Lights fade slowly and then come up again, it is brighter now, day is dawning

Bed number nine is now empty. Captain Selkirk is in his office with Nurse Penfold

Selkirk What you need now, Nurse, is rest. I can't have my nurses losing their beauty sleep, especially the pretty ones.

Nurse Penfold looks demur

How long have you been on duty now—nearly twenty-four hours?

Nurse I'm not the only one, sir.

Selkirk Ah, but Sister Hart and I are old hands at this. We know how to pace ourselves. (*He becomes serious*) Nurse, I have been very impressed with the way you dealt with the Underwood case. So, I know, has Sister, though she won't perhaps say so to you directly. I know it cannot have been easy for you but you have certainly come through with flying colours. How do you feel?

Nurse A little tired and ... I think I know what you meant, yesterday, about anger, sir. When a brave man dies ...

Captain Selkirk nods

Sister Hart enters and goes to Captain Selkirk's office

Sister Excuse me, sir, are there any urgent despatches you have for battalion headquarters, the messenger is waiting. (*She looks expectantly at him*)

Selkirk Thank you, Sister. No, nothing urgent. There was a paper to do with Private Underwood but his death has made it quite irrelevant. (*He slowly tears the paper into pieces*)

Sister Shall I tell the runner there is nothing to be sent to H.Q. today, sir?

Selkirk I would be very grateful if you would, Sister.

Sister Of course, sir.

Sister Hart leaves Captain Selkirk's office and exits offstage

Nurse Sir, would it seem impertinent for me to ask what the paper concerning Private Underwood was about?

Selkirk (*teasing*) Well, Nurse, I don't usually reveal military secrets to our nurses ...

Nurse I'm sorry, sir.

Selkirk Don't apologize, Nurse, I'm sure you're entitled to ask. The message was from one of Private Underwood's field officers ... it was a recommendation for promotion. ... Now I suggest you run along and get some rest. (*He stands*)

Nurse Thank you, sir.

Nurse Penfold leaves the office. Captain Selkirk's smile fades and he sinks into his chair, he is perplexed. Nurse Penfold crosses the ward

Sister Hart enters

Nurse Penfold, lost in her own thoughts, almost bumps into Sister Hart

Oh, I'm sorry, Sister.

Sister (*seeing Nurse Penfold is close to tears*) Nurse Penfold, you dealt very capably with your last patient, I hope you will not allow his death to unsettle you. I did warn you of the dangers of becoming too attached to your patients.

Nurse (*recovering herself*) I am sorry, Sister, it's just that when I heard that Private Underwood was to be commended for bravery it made me realize how tragic his death was.

Sister (*looking across at Captain Selkirk's office*) Of course ... I understand ... It is strange how often heroes see themselves as cowards ... Now, Nurse, before you go off duty you will help me prepare this bed for the next occupant. It will doubtless be needed before the day is out.

They go to bed number nine and begin to re-arrange it

Very slowly the Lights fade

The sound of a single bird singing can be heard, followed by the roar of guns

CURTAIN

FURNITURE AND PROPERTY LIST

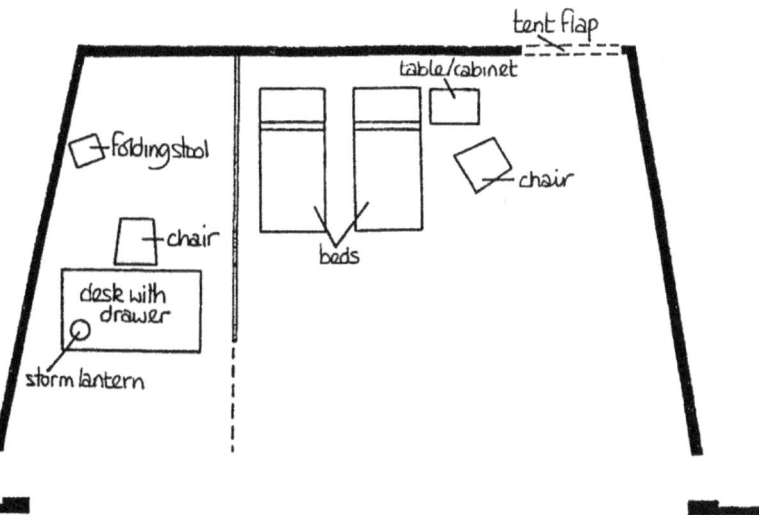

On stage: **Ward:**
Beds (of which only one need be authentic)
Chair. *On it:* basin with water and flannel in
Table or cabinet. *On it:* Water jug and enamel cup
Storm lanterns
Treatment sheet
Medical equipment

Office:
A roughly curtained off area
Table with drawer. *On it:* books, files and papers. Storm lantern. *In drawer:* flask containing whisky
Folding stool

Off stage: Bowl of soup and spoon **(Nurse)**
Towel **(Nurse)**
Requisition sheet **(Sister)**
Bowl and syringe **(Sister)**
Pencil and writing paper **(Nurse)**

LIGHTING PLOT

Practical fittings required: 2 Storm lanterns

Cue 1	As the CURTAIN rises bring up daytime lighting	(Page 1)
Cue 2	**Selkirk** drinks *Fade lighting for few seconds. Bring up lighting—twilight*	(Page 11)
Cue 3	**Nurse** takes **Private Underwood**'s hand *Fade lighting for few seconds. Bring up late evening lighting. The lanterns are lit*	(Page 12)
Cue 4	**Sister:** "... no longer alive." *Fade lighting for few seconds. Bring up night-time lighting*	(Page 14)
Cue 5	**Nurse** continually wipes **Private Underwood**'s face *Lights crossfade to Captain Selkirk's office*	(Page 14)
Cue 6	**Selkirk** drains the last drop from his flask *Lights crossfade to the ward*	(Page 15)
Cue 7	**Private Underwood** relaxes *Fade lights for few seconds. Bring up lighting on the ward*	(Page 15)
Cue 8	**Sister:** "... for being wounded." *Fade lights for few seconds. Bring up over-all lighting*	(Page 15)
Cue 9	**Sister** exits *Fade lights for few seconds. Bring up lighting*	(Page 17)
Cue 10	**Private Underwood** is slipping into unconsciousness *Fade lights for few seconds. Bring up lighting—daybreak*	(Page 18)
Cue 11	**Sister** and **Nurse** begin to re-arrange bed number nine *Fade lights slowly*	(Page 20)

EFFECTS PLOT

Intermittently throughout the play the rumble of gunfire can be heard, with the occasional loud salvo

The deafening roar of an artillery barrage precedes the opening of the play. Fade to give place to birdsong. Fade birdsong slowly

Cue 1   **Sister:** "... before the day is out."   (Page 20)
Single birdsong followed by roar of guns

www.ingramcontent.com/pod-product-compliance
Lightning Source LLC
Chambersburg PA
CBHW070455050426
42450CB00012B/3294